to Joyce Woods

from Raquel Mounce

For Joyce :
Given on 11-30-2000 - Thurs .
a special gift for Someone Special !
Love,
Raquel.

The Ruby Book of
LOVE

PUBLICATIONS INTERNATIONAL, LTD.

Photo credits: Front cover: **Walter Schmid/Tony Stone Images** (center); **Sacco Productions Limited/Chicago** (background).

FPG International: Color Box; David McGlynn; Benjamin Shearn; Telegraph Colour Library; VCG; **International Stock**: Willie Holdman; Edmund Nagele; Zeva Oelbaum; **SuperStock**.

Louis Weber, C.E.O.
Publications International, Ltd.
7373 North Cicero Ave.
Lincolnwood, Illinois 60646

Permission is never granted for commercial purposes.

Manufactured in China.

8 7 6 5 4 3 2 1

ISBN: 0-7853-3735-0

Original inspirations written by:

Elaine Creasman, Lain Chroust Ehmann, Margaret Anne Huffman, and Marie Jones.

Elaine Creasman is a writer and poet. She writes for a variety of inspirational magazines including *Guideposts* and *Decision.*

Lain Chroust Ehmann is a columnist for the *San Jose Mercury News.* She writes on inspirational topics for numerous publications.

Margaret Anne Huffman is an award-winning writer and journalist. She has authored and contributed to numerous titles including *Simple Wisdom, Graces,* and *Family Celebrations.*

Marie Jones is a published writer of fiction and non-fiction stories as well as the author of several screenplays.

Other quotations compiled by Cathy Ann Tell.

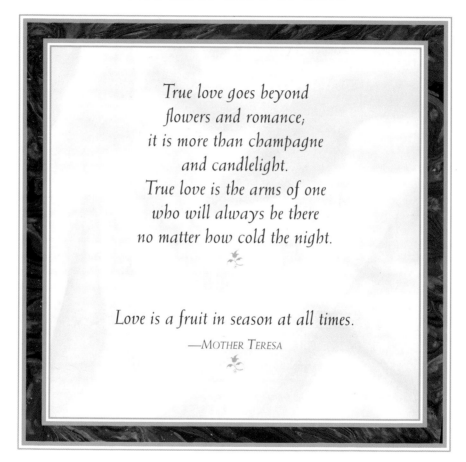

True love goes beyond
flowers and romance;
it is more than champagne
and candlelight.
True love is the arms of one
who will always be there
no matter how cold the night.

Love is a fruit in season at all times.

—MOTHER TERESA

Stand in a beloved's shade,
not shadow,
and discover new sights to share,
new directions to go,
all leading to even
more reasons for standing together.

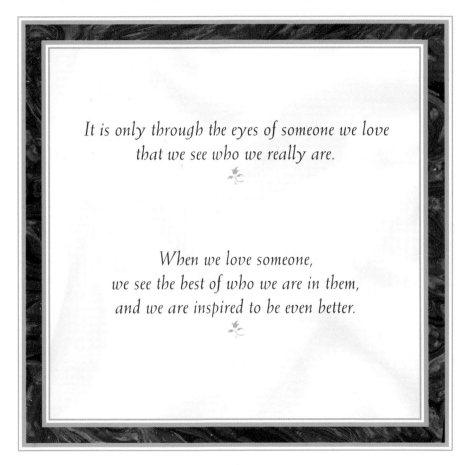

It is only through the eyes of someone we love
that we see who we really are.

When we love someone,
we see the best of who we are in them,
and we are inspired to be even better.

*Delicacy is to love
what grace is to beauty.*

—MADAME DE MAINTENON

*It's amazing how
the little things—
like your smile—
can lift my spirits
and remind me
I am loved.*

Love conquers all things:
let us too give in to Love.

—VIRGIL

To love me
is not to understand
everything about me
but to want to.

Geese take turns,
take up the slack,
in the natural rhythm of things.
By sharing our journey,
we, too, gain that updraft of air,
where we'll rest awhile,
knowing love is the wind under our wings.

Love is not a protective cage,
but the gift of wings that allow another to fly free.

There is no fear in love,
but perfect love casts out fear.

—1 JOHN 4:18

Two people in love
is a work of art—
a masterpiece sublime.
Two equal halves
that make a whole—
an image so divine.

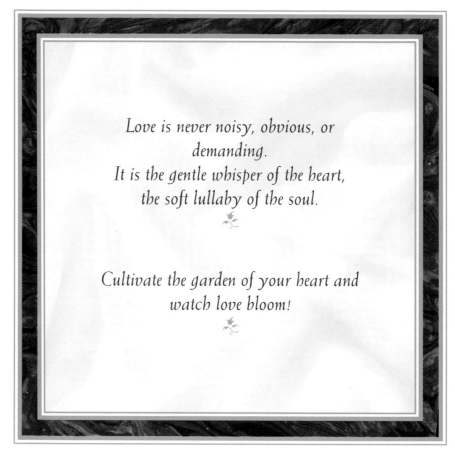

Love is never noisy, obvious, or
demanding.
It is the gentle whisper of the heart,
the soft lullaby of the soul.

Cultivate the garden of your heart and
watch love bloom!

Thank you, my love,
for trusting me enough
to tear down walls
of fear and doubt.
Thank you
for opening wide
the door of
your wounded heart
to let me love you.

*Loving, like prayer, is a power
as well as a process.
It's curative. It is creative.*

—ZONA GALE

*Honesty
Humility
Generosity
Patience—
four cornerstones
of love.*

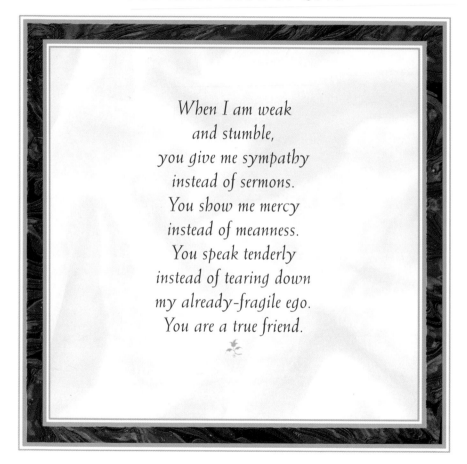

When I am weak
and stumble,
you give me sympathy
instead of sermons.
You show me mercy
instead of meanness.
You speak tenderly
instead of tearing down
my already-fragile ego.
You are a true friend.

Two persons love in another the future good
which they aid one another to unfold.

—MARGARET FULLER

If there were never
a broken heart,
we'd never know
the miracle
of love's healing power.

To love deeply in one direction
makes us more loving in all others.

—ANNE-SOPHIE SWETCHINE

How can I love God—
the originator and
the instigator
of all love?
If God is love,
and he is self-sufficient,
how can I possibly
show him I love him?
By receiving his love.

Love dictated by
"I will love you if . . ."
is not true love.
True love says,
"I will love you
even so."

Love is the glue that binds
two souls together
in common experiences,
shared goals, and mutual desires.

Our union, like an heirloom pewter teapot
or vintage walnut table,
grows more lovely and valuable
in the hands of daily use.

Love comforteth like sunshine after rain.

—WILLIAM SHAKESPEARE

True love is
surrendering
to the dictates
of my healed heart
and giving my all,
no matter what the risk,
no matter what the cost.

Loving sometimes means holding on,
and sometimes means letting go.
Trust your heart to know the time for each.

What is life without the radiance of love?

—J.C.F. VON SCHILLER

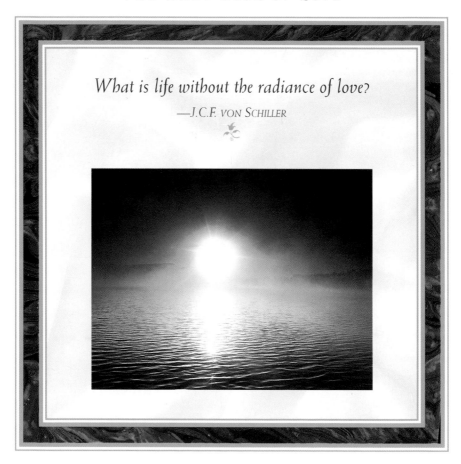

Today, I feel empty—
drained of love.
It's time to still
my heart and
open it up
to receive
all the love
that's being offered
to me.

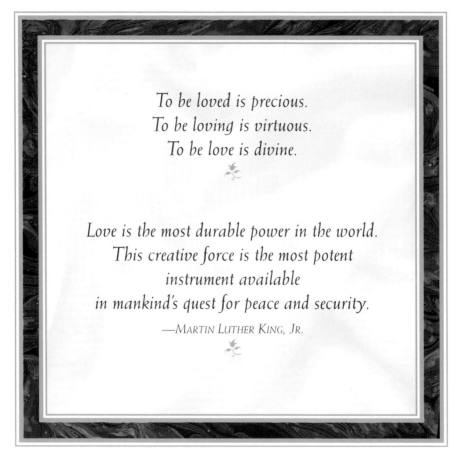

To be loved is precious.
To be loving is virtuous.
To be love is divine.

❧

Love is the most durable power in the world.
This creative force is the most potent
instrument available
in mankind's quest for peace and security.

—MARTIN LUTHER KING, JR.

❧

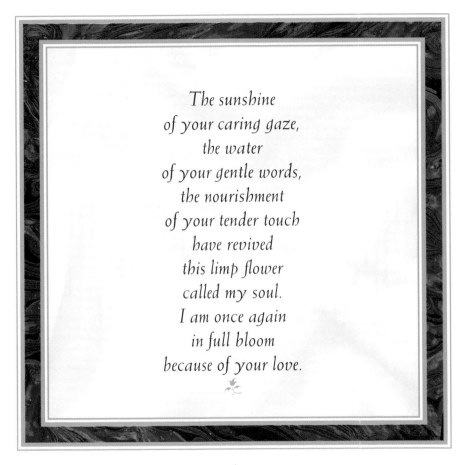

The sunshine
of your caring gaze,
the water
of your gentle words,
the nourishment
of your tender touch
have revived
this limp flower
called my soul.
I am once again
in full bloom
because of your love.

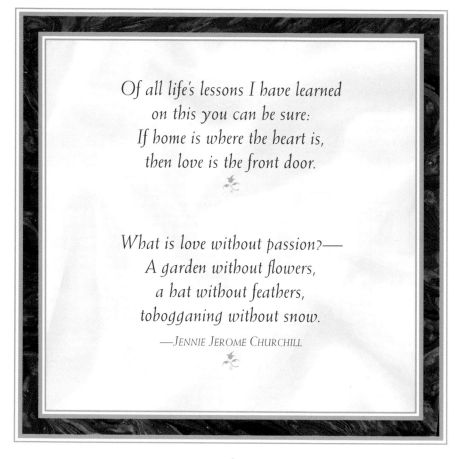

Of all life's lessons I have learned
on this you can be sure:
If home is where the heart is,
then love is the front door.

What is love without passion?—
A garden without flowers,
a hat without feathers,
tobogganing without snow.

—JENNIE JEROME CHURCHILL

When you hug me,
I feel safe—
encircled by your love.

To find love,
we think we must first find the courage
to take a big chance
by risking our heart to another;
yet it's only then that we discover
it's in the very act of offering ourselves
that love is found.

Love is all we have,
the only way that each can help the other.

—*EURIPIDES*

The path of love is never easy.
Yet it is in the ups and downs,
the times of trouble and need,
that together you forge a bond
strong enough to withstand
whatever the road ahead may bring.

Love is joining your soul with another's,
not for an hour, a month, or a year,
but for a lifetime.

The heart that loves is always young.

—GREEK PROVERB

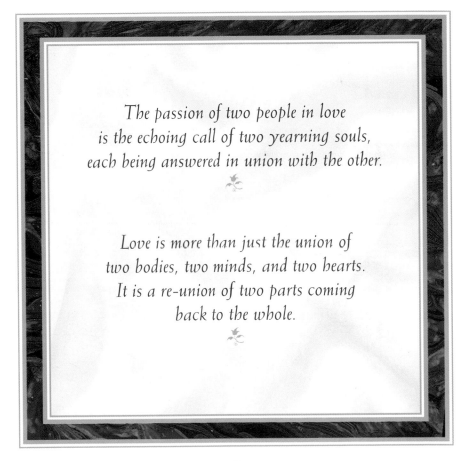

The passion of two people in love
is the echoing call of two yearning souls,
each being answered in union with the other.

Love is more than just the union of
two bodies, two minds, and two hearts.
It is a re-union of two parts coming
back to the whole.

Love is about knowing when it's time to lead
and when it's time to follow.
But mostly, it's about two people
walking through life side by side.

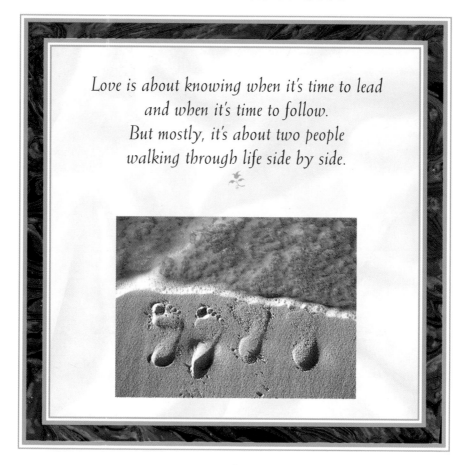

One word frees us of all the weight
and pain of life:
That word is love.

—SOPHOCLES

One of life's greatest sorrows
is love that is not returned.
One of life's greatest joys is
knowing that someone loves me
and is willing to complete
the circle of love.

The human heart is like a ship on a stormy sea
driven about by winds blowing
from all four corners of heaven.

—MARTIN LUTHER

The most important element of love is trust—
trust that you each hold the other's best interests
in your heart,
and trust in yourself
that you can open your life to another without
reservation.

To love means always to act with kindness
and in the best interests of the other person.
We may have to do things
that will hurt another,
but only out of necessity,
and only with the greatest
honesty and compassion.

Love is a great beautifier.

—LOUISA MAY ALCOTT

Real love is not isolating.
It opens doors, opens horizons,
and opens your heart.
Search for people who add to your life,
who give you more than you
would have without them.

Love comforts, never alarms;
Always heals, never harms.
Always grows, never diminishes;
Love begins, never finishes.

You know... nothing about the sort
of love of which I am capable.
Every atom of your flesh is as dear
to me as my own:
in pain and sickness it would still be dear.

—CHARLOTTE BRONTË

All, everything that I understand,
I understand only because I love.

—LEO TOLSTOY

*Love will find a way
to bridge this chasm
between us.
Let's hold on
to memories
of lovely, loving days
we have enjoyed,
and let's look forward
and believe
we will have more of them.*

Caring for another, by its very nature,
involves risk.
But what better risk to take than to love,
for the returns are unequaled.

Is there such thing as love at first sight?
Of course.
Yet even more important
than the elation of a new love
is the strength and endurance
of an old one.

Choose your loves
as much by what you can
help them become
as by what they can offer you.

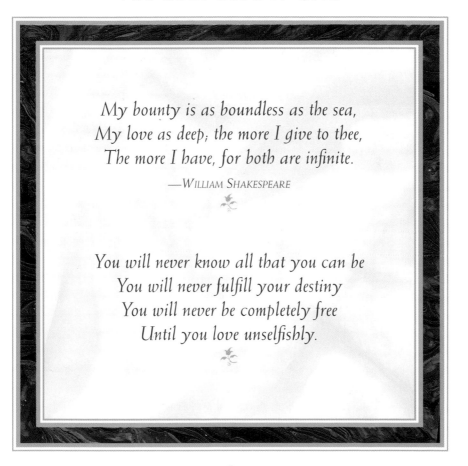

My bounty is as boundless as the sea,
My love as deep; the more I give to thee,
The more I have, for both are infinite.

—WILLIAM SHAKESPEARE

You will never know all that you can be
You will never fulfill your destiny
You will never be completely free
Until you love unselfishly.

Where love is concerned,
too much is not even enough.

—PIERRE-AUGUSTIN DE BEAUMARCHAIS

Anyone can fall in love.
Yet only those
with commitment and character
can make the everyday renewal
of that vow.

Love cannot be measured in a lab or proven in a textbook. Yet it, and it alone, is the substance of all things visible. Without love, there can be no creativity. Without creativity, there can be no life.

Never underestimate the power of a loving touch.

Falling in love is like opening all the doors,
pulling back all the curtains,
and flooding the dark room of our heart
with brilliant warmth and light.

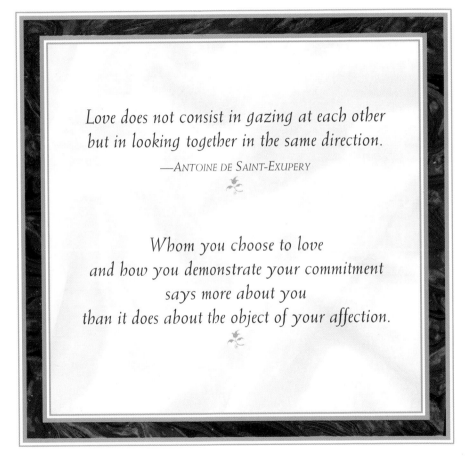

Love does not consist in gazing at each other
but in looking together in the same direction.
—ANTOINE DE SAINT-EXUPERY

Whom you choose to love
and how you demonstrate your commitment
says more about you
than it does about the object of your affection.

*Love makes up for the lack of long memories
by a sort of magic.
All other affections need a past:
love creates a past which envelops us,
as if by enchantment.*

—BENJAMIN CONSTANT

*To truly love someone is to see
them as they really are,
with all their faults, quirks, and defects,
and still see them as perfect
expressions of the Divine.*

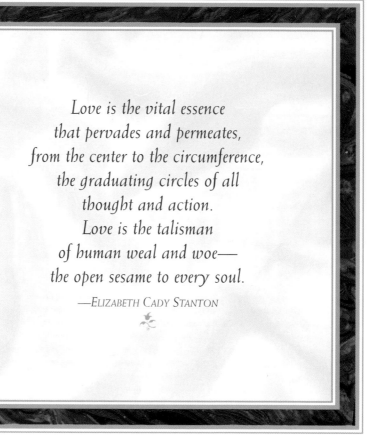

Love is the vital essence
that pervades and permeates,
from the center to the circumference,
the graduating circles of all
thought and action.
Love is the talisman
of human weal and woe—
the open sesame to every soul.

—ELIZABETH CADY STANTON

Love cannot be measured in pounds,
ounces, hours, or yards,
yet it grows larger all the same.
The only way to gauge its progress
is by sensing how much
your heart is expanding.

Love takes many shapes and forms,
each with its own personality.
Value and appreciate every one
for the special joy it brings to your life.

Love is an act of endless forgiveness,
a tender look which becomes a habit.

—PETER USTINOV

Love is where you seek it—
in the laughing eyes of a child,
in a garden lush with color,
in the soft warmth of a loved-one's
embrace.
There is no shortage of love
anywhere... only seekers.

Beloved, let us love one another,
because love is from God;
everyone who loves is born of God.

—1 JOHN 4:7

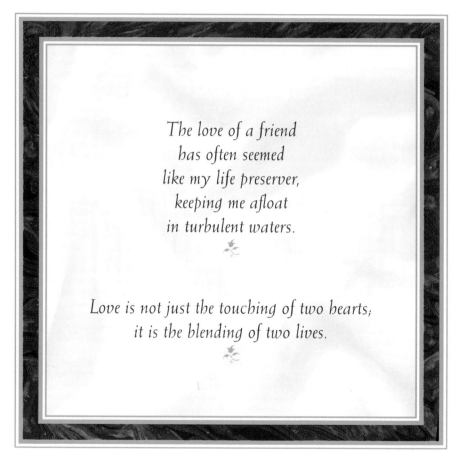

The love of a friend
has often seemed
like my life preserver,
keeping me afloat
in turbulent waters.

Love is not just the touching of two hearts;
it is the blending of two lives.

And now faith, hope, and love abide,
these three;
and the greatest of these is love.

—1 CORINTHIANS 13:13